THE LITTLE
DESSERT
Cookbook

THE LITTLE
DESSERT
COOKBOOK

ULTIMATE
EDITIONS

First published by Ultimate Editions in 1996

© 1996 Anness Publishing Limited

Ultimate Editions is an imprint of
Anness Publishing Limited
Boundary Row Studios
I Boundary Row
London SEI 8HP

ISBN I 86035 156 5

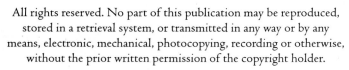

Publisher Joanna Lorenz
Senior Cookery Editor Linda Fraser
Assistant Editor Emma Brown
Designer Patrick McLeavey
Illustrator Anna Koska
Photographers Karl Adamson, Don Last,
James Duncan, Steve Baxter, Amanda Heywood &
Edward Allwright
Recipes Christine France, Carole Clements, Elizabeth Wolf-
Cohen, Carla Capalbo, Sarah Gates, Laura Washburn,
Steven Wheeler, Shirley Gill & Norma MacMillan

For all recipes, quantities are given in both metric and imperial
measures, and, where appropriate, measures are also given in
standard cups and spoons. Follow one set, but not a mixture,
because they are not interchangeable.

Printed in China

Contents

Introduction

The strong-willed reach resolutely for the fruit bowl at the conclusion of every meal, but most of us  look hopefully at the host or hostess and dream about dessert. Cool and creamy, tart and fruity, or simply sinful, desserts are destined to remain on the menu.

Whatever the weather or season, there's a perfect pudding waiting in the wings, whether it be a comforting Blackberry Cobbler to chase away autumn blues or scoops of Hazelnut Ice Cream to celebrate summer. Friends will flip for Cherry Pancakes and children cheerfully eat their greens if a Black Forest Sundae or a slice of gloriously gooey French Chocolate Cake is in the offing.

When planning a menu, choose a dessert that will complement the preceding courses. A big, hearty casserole calls for a simple sorbet or fruit salad; a plainly grilled fish dish could lead to something really rich and creamy, such as Amaretto Soufflé or Minted Raspberry Bavarois. If you really want to push the boat out and serve a sumptuous sweet such as Hazelnut Meringue Torte with Pears, then keep the rest of the meal as low key as possible.

When serving eight or more, it is a good idea to offer a choice of desserts. These should contrast in terms of colour and content: a fruity Autumn Pudding (a sort of late harvest summer pudding) with Chocolate Loaf with Coffee Sauce, perhaps. Where appropriate, offer a choice of accompaniments, such as Greek-style yogurt and clotted cream.

For those guests who prefer fresh fruit, take a tip from Thai cookery. Cut fresh pineapple, melon and papaya into similar-sized wedges and overlap them on a decorative platter, with orange and pink grapefruit segments around the rim. Decorate with nasturtiums. Alternatively, slice a melon in half, using a zig-zag cut and easing it apart gently. Remove the seeds, then scoop out the flesh with a melon baller. Scrape out any remaining melon, then pile the balls back in the half-shell and drizzle with kirsch, Cointreau or Grand Marnier. Add a sprig of mint.

Decorating desserts is approaching an art form. A mousse surrounded by a fresh fruit coulis feathered with cream looks exquisite, while rosettes of cream spiked with chocolate leaves would make the perfect topping for a rich mocha mousse. Echo the main ingredient in the dessert, decorating a strawberry cheesecake with chocolate-tipped strawberries or Oranges in Caramel Sauce with strips of blanched orange peel. You can even present a dessert in an edible container, as when chocolate cups are filled with a liqueur-flavoured cream, or impress your guests with Summer Fruit Salad Ice Cream served in an ice bowl that would rival the finest crystal.

This recipe collection ranges from fruity desserts to classic custards, and also includes favourites like Creole Bread and Butter Pudding, Baked Caramel Custard and delicious Cherry Batter Pudding. Chocoholics get a chapter to themselves, and with a White Chocolate Cheesecake, a Chocolate Pavlova and Chocolate Cream Puffs on offer, you may be sure everyone will get more than their just desserts!

7

Ingredients

BUTTER

Use unsalted butter for desserts. Store it in the fridge, in the original wrapper. Freeze unopened packets in a polythene bag for up to six months.

CHOCOLATE

Most supermarkets stock a good range of chocolate and chocolate products, including sprinkles, chips and buttons. For the best results in cooking, use chocolate with a cocoa solid content of at least 50 per cent.

CREAM

Single cream has 18 per cent butterfat and is mainly used for pouring. In whipping cream the butterfat content increases to 35–38 per cent. When whipped, the cream will hold its shape briefly, but for a dessert decoration, use double cream (48 per cent butterfat).

EGGS

Unless recipes specify otherwise, use size 3 eggs. Always buy eggs from a reputable supplier, preferably date-stamped, and use them fresh. This is particularly important when the eggs in a recipe are not cooked.

GELATINE

Powdered gelatine is convenient and easy to use. A 15g/½oz/1 tbsp sachet sets 600ml/1 pint/2½ cups of liquid. Gelatine must be thoroughly dissolved before use. This is usually done by first softening it in cold water until spongy, then heating the mixture gently, stirring constantly. Vegetarian alternatives to gelatine are also widely available

SUGAR

Caster sugar is used for most desserts, as it dissolves quickly, but granulated sugar is preferred for caramel.

Decorations

ALMONDS

Flaked and nibbed almonds, plain or toasted, look good on creamy desserts. Gently press them on to the exposed sides of a cold soufflé for a delectable, crunchy coating.

CHOCOLATE CARAQUE

Pour melted chocolate on to a clean smooth surface, such as a marble slab. When set, draw a broad-bladed cook's knife lightly across the chocolate at an angle of 45°, to cut thin layers that curl into scrolls. For cheats' caraque use a potato peeler on a bar of plain or milk chocolate.

CHOCOLATE LEAVES

Select clean, unblemished, non-poisonous leaves (rose leaves work well) and brush the undersides evenly with melted chocolate. Leave to set on non-stick baking paper, then carefully peel away the chocolate leaves from the green leaves.

ICING SUGAR/COCOA POWDER

Lay strips of paper over a dessert before dusting it with icing sugar and/or cocoa powder. Carefully remove the paper to give a striped effect.

PIPED CHOCOLATE

Pipe melted chocolate designs on non-stick baking paper. Spider webs, hearts and stars all look good, but lift them very carefully when transferring them to a cake or pudding.

WHIPPED CREAM

Swirls, shells and rosettes of whipped cream are easy to achieve. Use a piping bag fitted with a large, star-shaped nozzle and keep the pressure even. Take care not to overwhip cream for piping — the cream will thicken further as it is forced out of the piping bag. Practice makes perfect — try practising your piping technique using a cheap alternative to cream, such as instant mashed potato!

FRUIT AND FLOWERS

Frosted grapes — made by brushing grapes with water, then dusting them in caster sugar — look lovely. Fresh rose petals can't be eaten, but look great surrounding a summery sweet. Berry fruits like strawberries and raspberries make perfect decorations, as do tiny sprigs of redcurrants.

9

Techniques

WHIPPING CREAM

Cooks with strong wrists swear that a rotary whisk gives the greatest volume, but a hand-held electric mixer works well. Use double cream for decorations, and be careful not to overwhip the cream. It should just hold its shape and must not look grainy.

MELTING CHOCOLATE

The best way to melt chocolate is over very hot but not boiling water. Break the chocolate into a heatproof bowl. Bring a saucepan of water to the boil, turn off the heat and set the bowl on top. Stir as the chocolate melts. Do not add any liquid to melting chocolate.

FLIPPING A PANCAKE

Pancakes are child's play if you use a good pan, grease it just sufficiently to prevent the batter from sticking, and pour in only enough batter to coat the base evenly. As the pancake sets, shiver the pan to keep it from sticking. Check that it is lightly brown underneath, then hold the pan handle firmly, slide the pancake forward to the opposite rim and flip it over towards you with a neat flick of your wrist.

WHISKING EGG WHITES

Bowl and whisk must be clean, dry and completely grease-free. Separate the eggs carefully; if there is any yolk with the whites they will not whisk successfully. Beat gently until foamy, then increase the speed and continue whisking until the whites are stiff enough to hold their shape. When adding whisked whites to a stiff mixture, stir in a couple of spoonfuls to lighten it, then fold in the rest.

MAKING CHOCOLATE CASES

Little chocolate cases make perfect containers for mousses and whips. Use double cupcake cases or sweet cases. Using a brush or teaspoon, coat the inside of the inner case evenly with melted chocolate, invert, and leave to set. Peel away the paper and fill just before serving.

PREPARING A SOUFFLE DISH

To make a cold soufflé which looks as though it has risen above the dish, use a smaller-than-necessary soufflé dish, adding a paper collar to hold the excess mixture in place. Cut a piece of non-stick baking paper slightly longer than the circumference of the dish and three times its depth. Fold it over lengthways, wrap it tightly around the outside of the dish and secure it firmly in place with string or freezer tape.

11

MAKING AN ICE BOWL

Ice creams and sorbets look spectacular in an ice bowl. Choose two freezerproof bowls, one about 7.5cm/3in wider than the other. Pour water into the larger bowl to two-thirds full, then centre the small bowl inside it, weighting it so that it floats level with the big bowl. Keep it in place with masking tape. Top up the water, then freeze, adding flowers or leaves when the water is semi-frozen. Carefully release the ice bowl once frozen and store in the freezer.

COOK'S TIP

It is not really necessary to make a paper collar for a hot soufflé. Instead, run a clean knife around the edge of the mixture, at a depth of 1cm/½in, to encourage even rising.

Fruit Desserts

Autumn Pudding

INGREDIENTS

10 slices white or brown bread, at least 1 day old
1 Bramley cooking apple, peeled, cored and sliced
225g/8oz ripe red plums, halved and stoned
225g/8oz/2 cups blackberries
60ml/4 tbsp water
75g/3oz/6 tbsp caster sugar
yogurt or fromage frais, to serve

SERVES 6

1 Slice off the crusts from the bread and use a biscuit cutter to stamp out a 7.5cm/3in round from one slice. Cut all the remaining slices in half.

2 Put the bread round in the base of a 1.2 litre/ 2 pint/5 cup pudding basin, then overlap the halves around the sides, saving some for the top.

3 Place the fruit, water and sugar in a pan, heat gently until the sugar dissolves, then simmer for 10 minutes, until soft. Drain, reserving the juice.

4 Spoon the fruit into the basin. Top with the reserved bread and spoon over the reserved juice.

5 Cover the basin with a saucer and place a weight on top of it. Chill the pudding overnight. Turn out on to a serving plate and serve with yogurt or fromage frais.

Cherry Pancakes

INGREDIENTS

PANCAKES
50g/2oz/½ cup plain flour
50g/2oz/½ cup plain wholemeal flour
pinch of salt
1 egg white
150ml/¼ pint/⅔ cup milk
150ml/¼ pint/⅔ cup water
a little oil for frying
fromage frais, to serve
FILLING
425g/15oz can black cherries in juice
7.5ml/1½ tsp arrowroot

SERVES 4

1 Sift the flours and salt into a bowl, adding any bran left in the sieve to the bowl.

2 Make a well in the centre of the flour and add the egg white. Gradually beat in the milk and water, whisking hard until all the flour and liquid is incorporated and the batter is smooth and bubbly.

3 Heat a non-stick pan with a small amount of oil until it is very hot. Pour in just enough batter to cover the base of the pan and swirl to cover it evenly.

4 Cook until the pancake is set and golden, and then turn to cook the other side. Remove to a sheet of kitchen paper and cook the remaining batter, to make about eight pancakes in all.

5 Drain the cherries, reserving the juice. Blend about 30ml/2 tbsp of the juice from the can of cherries with the arrowroot in a saucepan. Stir in the rest of the juice. Heat gently, stirring, until boiling. Stir the mixture over a moderate heat for about 2 minutes, until thickened and clear.

6 Add the cherries to the pan and stir until heated through. Spoon the cherry mixture into the pancakes, fold them in quarters and serve with fromage frais.

Poached Pears in Maple-yogurt Sauce

INGREDIENTS

6 firm dessert pears
15ml/1 tbsp lemon juice
250ml/8fl oz/1 cup sweet white wine or cider
thinly pared rind of 1 lemon
1 cinnamon stick
30ml/2 tbsp maple syrup
2.5ml/½ tsp arrowroot
150ml/¼ pint/⅔ cup Greek yogurt

SERVES 6

1 Thinly peel the pears, leaving them whole and with the stalks on. Brush with lemon juice, to prevent them from browning. Using a potato peeler or small knife, scoop out the core from the base of each pear and discard it.

2 Place the pears in a wide, heavy-based saucepan and pour over the wine, with enough cold water to almost cover the pears.

3 Add the pared lemon rind and cinnamon stick, then bring to the boil. Reduce the heat, cover the pan and simmer for about 30–40 minutes, or until all the pears are tender. Turn them occasionally so that they cook evenly. Lift out the pears carefully, with a large spoon, draining them well.

4 Bring the remaining liquid to the boil. Boil, uncovered, to reduce to about 120ml/4fl oz/ ½ cup. Strain, and add the maple syrup. Blend some of the liquid with the arrowroot. Return to the pan and cook, stirring, until thick and clear. Cool.

5 Slice each pear about three-quarters of the way through, leaving the slices attached at the stem end. Fan out each pear on a serving plate.

6 Stir 30ml/2 tbsp of the cooled syrup into the Greek yogurt and spoon it around each pear on the plates. Drizzle with the remaining syrup and serve the pears immediately.

Oranges in Caramel Sauce

3 Using a sharp vegetable knife, slice all the peeled fruit crossways into rounds about 1cm/½in thick. Put the orange slices in a serving bowl and pour over any juice.

4 Half-fill a large bowl with cold water and set aside. Place the sugar and 45ml/3 tbsp water in a small heavy-based pan without a non-stick coating. Bring it to the  boil over a high heat, swirling the pan to dissolve all the sugar. Boil, without stirring, until the mixture turns a dark caramel colour. Remove the pan from the heat and, standing well back, dip the base of the pan into the bowl of cold water in order to stop the cooking process.

5 Add 30ml/2 tbsp water to the caramel, pouring it down the sides of the pan, and swirling it to mix it thoroughly. Add the strips of orange rind and return the pan to the heat. Simmer over a medium-low heat for 8–10 minutes until the orange strips are slightly translucent, stirring occasionally.

6 Pour the caramel and rind over the orange slices in the serving bowl, turn gently to mix everything together and chill for at least 1 hour before serving.

INGREDIENTS

6 large unwaxed seedless oranges
90g/3½oz/½ cup granulated sugar

SERVES 6

1 Using a vegetable peeler, remove wide strips of rind from two of the oranges. Stack two or three strips on top of each other and cut them into very thin julienne strips.

2 Cut a slice from the top and the base of each orange. Cut off the peel in strips from the top to the base, following the contours of the fruit.

17

Apples & Raspberries in Rose Pouchong Syrup

INGREDIENTS

5ml / 1 tsp rose pouchong tea
5ml / 1 tsp rose water (optional)
50g / 2oz / ¼ cup granulated sugar
5ml / 1 tsp lemon juice
5 dessert apples
175g / 6oz / 1 cup fresh raspberries

SERVES 4

3 Peel, core and quarter the apples. Poach them in the syrup for about 5 minutes, then transfer the apples and syrup to a large metal tray and leave to cool.

4 Pour the cooled apples and rose pouchong syrup into a mixing bowl and add the fresh raspberries. Mix together well to combine all the ingredients, then spoon the fruit mixture into individual serving dishes or bowls and serve at room temperature.

1 Warm a large teapot. Add the tea and 900ml/ 1½ pints/3¾ cups of boiling water together with the rose water, if liked. Allow to infuse for 4 minutes.

2 Place the sugar and lemon juice in a large stainless steel saucepan. Carefully strain in all the infused rose pouchong tea and stir well until the sugar dissolves.

COOK'S TIP

If fresh raspberries are out of season, use the same weight of frozen fruit or a 400g/14oz can of fruit, drained well.

Fresh Fruit with Mango Sauce

INGREDIENTS

1 large ripe mango, peeled, stoned and chopped
rind of 1 unwaxed orange
juice of 3 oranges
caster sugar, to taste
2 peaches
2 nectarines
1 small mango, peeled
2 plums
1 pear or ½ small melon
juice of 1 lemon
25-50g/1-2oz/2 heaped tbsp wild
strawberries (optional)
25-50g/1-2oz/2 heaped tbsp raspberries
25-50g/1-2oz/2 heaped tbsp blueberries
small mint sprigs, to decorate

SERVES 6

1 In a food processor fitted with a metal blade, process the large mango until smooth. Add the orange rind, juice and sugar to taste and process again until very smooth. Press through a sieve into a bowl. Chill the sauce until needed.

2 Peel the peaches, if liked, then stone and slice the peaches, nectarines, small mango and plums. Peel and quarter the pear, if using, and remove the core. Alternatively, deseed and slice the half melon thinly and remove all the peel.

3 Place all the sliced fruits on a large plate and sprinkle with the lemon juice to prevent any of them from dis-colouring. Chill the plate of fruit, covered with clear film, for up to 3 hours before completing the preparation for serving.

4 To serve the fruits, arrange the slices on individ-ual serving plates and spoon the strawberries, if using, raspberries and blueberries over the top. Drizzle with a little of the fresh mango sauce and decorate the plates with mint sprigs. Serve the remaining mango sauce separately.

Jellies & Ices

Rhubarb & Orange Water-ice

1 Trim the rhubarb and slice it into 2.5cm/1in lengths. Place it in a pan.

2 Finely grate the rind from the orange and squeeze out all the juice. Add all the rind and about half the orange juice to the rhubarb in the pan and simmer until  the rhubarb becomes just tender. Stir in the clear honey until completely dissolved.

3 Heat the remaining orange juice and stir in the gelatine to dissolve it. Stir it into the rhubarb. Turn the whole mixture into a rigid freezer container and freeze it for about 2 hours until slushy.

4 Take the mixture out of the freezer and beat it with an electric mixer, to break up all the ice crystals. Return the water-ice to the freezer and freeze until firm. Leave  the water-ice to soften slightly at room temperature before serving, decorated with orange slices.

23

INGREDIENTS

350g/12oz pink rhubarb
1 orange
15ml/1 tbsp clear honey
5ml/1 tsp powdered gelatine
orange slices, to decorate

SERVES 4

Black Forest Sundae

INGREDIENTS

400g/14oz can stoned black cherries in syrup
15ml/1 tbsp cornflour
45ml/3 tbsp kirsch
150ml/¼ pint/⅔ cup whipping cream
15ml/1 tbsp icing sugar
600ml/1 pint/2½ cups chocolate ice cream
115g/4oz chocolate cake
8 fresh cherries, to decorate

SERVES 4

4 Place a spoonful of the cooled cherries in the bottom of four sundae glasses, then continue with layers of ice cream, chocolate cake, whipped cream and more cherries until the glasses are full.

5 Finish each glass with a piece of chocolate cake, two scoops of ice cream and more whipped cream. Decorate with the fresh cherries.

1 Strain all but 30ml/2 tbsp of the cherry syrup into a saucepan. Measure the cornflour into a small bowl, add all the remaining syrup and mix well.

2 Bring the syrup in the saucepan to the boil. Stir in the cornflour and syrup mixture and simmer briefly to thicken. Add the cherries, stir in the kirsch and spread on to a metal tray to cool.

3 Using an electric mixer, whip the cream with the icing sugar until firm.

24

Hazelnut Ice Cream

1 Spread the hazelnuts on a baking sheet, and grill for 5 minutes, shaking the sheet frequently. Remove and cool, then place on a clean dish towel, and rub to remove the outer skin. Chop finely, or grind in a food processor with 30ml/2 tbsp of the sugar.

2 Heat the milk in a small pan with the vanilla pod until small bubbles appear on the surface. Remove the pan from the heat. Beat the egg yolks with a wire whisk or electric mixer. Gradually beat in the remaining sugar, and beat for about 5 minutes more until the mixture is pale yellow. Gradually strain in the vanilla milk, discarding the vanilla pod. Stir constantly until all the milk has been added.

3 Pour the mixture into the top of a double-boiler, or into a bowl placed over a pan of simmering water. Add the nuts. Stir over a moderate heat until the water in  the pan is boiling, and the custard thickens enough to coat the back of a spoon lightly. Remove from the heat and allow to cool.

4 Freeze in an ice-cream maker or in a plastic tub, beating several times during freezing to break up the ice crystals. Soften slightly before serving.

INGREDIENTS

75g/3oz/scant ½ cup hazelnuts
75g/3oz/6 tbsp granulated sugar
475ml/16fl oz/2 cups milk
10cm/4in piece of vanilla pod
4 egg yolks

SERVES 4–6

Frozen Apple & Blackberry Terrine

INGREDIENTS

450g / 1lb cooking or eating apples
300ml / ½ pint / 1¼ cups sweet cider
15ml / 1 tbsp clear honey
5ml / 1 tsp vanilla essence
*225g / 8oz / 2 cups fresh or frozen and
thawed blackberries*
15ml / 1 tbsp / 1 sachet powdered gelatine
2 egg whites
fresh apple slices and blackberries, to decorate

SERVES 6

1 Peel, core and chop the apples and place them in a pan, with half the cider. Bring the cider to the boil, then cover the pan and let the apples simmer gently until tender.

2 Turn the apples into a food processor or blender and process them to a smooth purée. Stir in the honey and vanilla essence. Add half the blackberries to half the apple purée, and then process again until smooth. Sieve to remove the pips.

3 Heat the remaining cider until almost boiling, then sprinkle the powdered gelatine over and stir until it has completely dissolved. Add half the cider and gelatine to the plain apple purée and the other half to the blackberry and apple purée.

4 Leave the purées to cool until almost set. Whisk the egg whites until they are stiff. Quickly fold them into the apple purée. Remove half of this purée to another bowl. Stir the remaining whole blackberries into the rest of the apple purée, then turn this into a 1.75 litre/3 pint/7½ cup loaf tin and pack it down firmly.

5 Top with the blackberry purée and spread it evenly. Finally, add the reserved apple purée and smooth it evenly. If necessary, freeze each layer until firm before adding the next.

6 Freeze the layered terrine until firm. To serve, allow it to stand at room temperature for 20 minutes so that it softens slightly. Turn it out of the loaf tin and, using a sharp knife, cut it into even-size slices. Serve the terrine decorated with fresh apple slices and a few fresh blackberries.

26

Coffee Jellies with Amaretti Cream

INGREDIENTS

75g/3oz/6 tbsp caster sugar
450ml/¾ pint/scant 2 cups hot strong coffee
30-45ml/2-3 tbsp dark rum or coffee liqueur
20ml/4 tsp powdered gelatine
COFFEE AMARETTI CREAM
150ml/¼ pint/⅔ cup double or
whipping cream
15ml/1 tbsp icing sugar, sifted
10-15ml/2-3 tsp instant coffee granules
dissolved in 15ml/1 tbsp hot water
6 large amaretti biscuits, crushed

SERVES 4

1 Put the sugar in a saucepan with 75ml/5 tbsp water and stir over a gentle heat until dissolved. Increase the heat; allow the syrup to boil steadily, without stirring, for 3–4 minutes.

2 Stir all the hot coffee and rum or coffee liqueur into the hot syrup. Sprinkle the powdered gelatine over the top and stir until it dissolves completely.

3 Pour the coffee jelly mixture into four wetted 150ml/¼ pint/⅔ cup moulds and allow them to cool thoroughly, before placing them in the fridge. Leave the jellies in the fridge for several hours until they are completely set.

4 To make the amaretti cream, lightly whip the cream with the icing sugar until it holds stiff peaks. Stir in the instant coffee, then gently fold in all but 30ml/2 tbsp of the crushed amaretti biscuits.

5 Remove the jellies from their moulds and place on four individual serving plates. Spoon a little of the coffee amaretti cream to one side of each jelly. Dust over the reserved amaretti biscuit crumbs and serve the dessert at once.

Grapes in Grape-yogurt Jelly

INGREDIENTS

200g / 7oz / 1½ cups white seedless grapes
450ml / ¾ pint / scant 2 cups white grape juice
15ml / 1 tbsp / 1 sachet powdered gelatine
120ml / 4fl oz / ½ cup natural yogurt

SERVES 4

1 Reserve four sprigs of grapes for decoration and then cut the rest in half.

2 Divide the grapes between four stemmed glasses and tilt the glasses on one side, propping them firmly in a bowl of ice.

3 Place the grape juice in a pan and heat it until almost boiling. Remove from the heat and sprinkle the powdered gelatine over it, stirring until it all dissolves.

4 Pour half the grape juice over the grapes in the tilted glasses and allow to set.

5 Cool the remaining grape juice but do not allow to set, then stir it into the yogurt.

6 Stand the four set glasses upright and divide the yogurt mixture among them. Chill to set, then top each one with a sprig of grapes before serving.

Summer Fruit Salad Ice Cream

INGREDIENTS

800g / 1¾lb / 7 cups mixed soft summer fruit,
such as raspberries, strawberries,
blackcurrants, redcurrants, etc.
2 eggs
250ml / 8fl oz / 1 cup Greek yogurt
175ml / 6fl oz / ¾ cup red grape juice
15ml / 1 tbsp / 1 sachet powdered gelatine

SERVES 6

1 Reserve half the fruit and purée the rest in a food processor or blender, or press it through a sieve to make a smooth purée.

2 Separate the eggs and whisk the yolks and the yogurt into the fruit purée.

3 Heat the grape juice until almost boiling, and then remove from the heat. Sprinkle the powdered gelatine over the juice and stir to dissolve completely.

4 Remove the dissolved gelatine mixture from the heat and whisk it into the fruit purée until well combined. Pour all this mixture into a plastic freezer container. Freeze the fruit purée until half-frozen and slushy in consistency.

5 Using a hand beater or electric mixer, whisk the egg whites until stiff peaks form. Quickly fold them into the half-frozen ice cream mixture.

6 Return the ice cream mixture to the freezer and freeze until almost firm. Serve it in scoops on small plates, decorated with the reserved soft fruits.

Mousses, Custards & Soufflés

Luxury Mocha Mousse

INGREDIENTS

225g / 8oz fine quality plain chocolate, chopped
60ml / 4 tbsp espresso or strong coffee
25g / 1oz / 2 tbsp butter, cut into pieces
30ml / 2 tbsp brandy or rum
3 eggs, separated
pinch of salt
40g / 1½oz / 3 tbsp caster sugar
120ml / 4fl oz / ½ cup whipping cream
30ml / 2 tbsp coffee-flavour liqueur
chocolate coffee beans, to decorate (optional)

SERVES 6

1 In a saucepan over a medium heat, melt the plain chocolate in the coffee, stirring frequently until smooth. Remove from the heat and beat in the butter and brandy or rum.

2 In a small bowl, beat the egg yolks lightly, then whisk in the melted chocolate; the mixture will thicken. Set aside to cool. In a large bowl, beat the egg whites with an electric mixer to "break" them. Add a pinch of salt and beat on a medium speed until soft peaks form. Increase the speed and beat until stiff peaks form. Beat in the sugar, 15ml / 1 tbsp at a time, beating well after each addition until the egg whites are glossy and stiff, but not dry.

3 Mix a large spoonful of whites into the chocolate mixture to lighten it, then fold the chocolate into the remaining whites. Pour into 6 individual dishes or a large glass serving bowl and chill for at least 3–4 hours, until set, before serving.

4 In a medium bowl, beat the cream and coffee-flavour liqueur until soft peaks form. Spoon into an icing bag fitted with a medium star tip and pipe rosettes or shells on to the surface of the mousse. Decorate with chocolate coffee beans, if liked.

Baked Caramel Custard

INGREDIENTS

250g/9oz/scant 1¼ cups granulated sugar
60ml/4 tbsp water
1 vanilla pod
400ml/14fl oz/1⅔ cups milk
250ml/8fl oz/1 cup whipping cream
5 large eggs
2 egg yolks

SERVES 6–8

34

1 Put 175g/6oz/¾ cup of the sugar in a small heavy saucepan with the water to moisten. Bring to the boil over a high heat, swirling the pan until the sugar dissolves. Boil, without stirring, until the syrup turns a dark caramel colour (this will take about 4–5 minutes).

2 Immediately pour the caramel into a 1 litre/1¾ pint/4 cup soufflé dish. Holding the dish with oven gloves, quickly swirl the dish to coat the base and sides with the caramel and set aside. (The caramel will harden quickly as it cools.) Place the dish in a small roasting tin. Preheat the oven to 160°C/325°F/Gas 3.

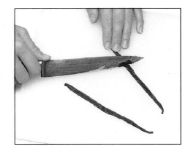

3 Split the vanilla pod lengthways and scrape the black seeds into a saucepan. Add the milk and cream. Bring to the boil over a medium-high heat, stirring frequently. Remove the pan from the heat, cover and set aside for 15–20 minutes.

4 In a bowl, whisk the eggs and egg yolks with the remaining sugar for 2–3 minutes until smooth and creamy. Whisk in the hot milk. Strain the mixture into the caramel-lined dish. Cover with foil.

5 Pour enough boiling water into the roasting tin to come halfway up the sides of the dish. Bake the custard for 40–45 minutes until a knife inserted about 5cm/2in from the edge comes out clean (the custard should be just set). Remove from the roasting tin and cool for at least 30 minutes, then chill overnight.

6 To turn out, carefully run a sharp knife around the edge of the dish to loosen the custard. Cover the dish with an upturned plate. Holding them both tightly, invert the dish and plate together. Gently lift one edge of the dish, allowing the caramel to run over the sides, then slowly lift off the dish.

Minted Raspberry Bavarois

INGREDIENTS

*450g / 1lb / 3 cups fresh or frozen and
thawed raspberries
30ml / 2 tbsp icing sugar
30ml / 2 tbsp lemon juice
15ml / 1 tbsp finely chopped fresh mint
30ml / 2 tbsp powdered gelatine
75ml / 5 tbsp boiling water
300ml / ½ pint / 1¼ cups custard
300ml / ½ pint / 1¼ cups Greek yogurt
fresh mint sprigs, to decorate*

SERVES 6

3 Sprinkle 5ml/ 1 tsp of gelatine over 30ml/2 tbsp of boiling water and stir until it has dissolved. Add it to 150ml/¼ pint/ ⅔ cup of the raspberry fruit purée.

4 Pour this jelly into a 1 litre/1¾ pint/4 cup mould, and leave the mould to chill in the fridge until the jelly is just on the point of setting. Tip the mould to swirl the setting jelly around the sides, then leave to chill until the jelly has set completely.

1 Reserve some raspberries for decoration. Place the rest with the icing sugar and lemon juice in a food processor or blender. Process until smooth.

5 Stir the rest of the fruit purée into the custard with the yogurt. Dissolve the rest of the gelatine in the rest of the water and stir it into the fruit.

2 Pass the purée through a sieve to remove the raspberry seeds. Add the chopped fresh mint. You should have about 600ml/1 pint/2½ cups of purée.

6 Pour the custard into the mould and leave to chill until it has set. To serve, dip the mould quickly into hot water, then turn it out and decorate it with the reserved raspberries and the mint sprigs.

Baked Custard with Burnt Sugar

INGREDIENTS

1 vanilla pod
1 litre / 1¾ pints / 4 cups double cream
6 egg yolks
115g / 4oz / ½ cup caster sugar
30ml / 2 tbsp almond or orange liqueur
75g / 3oz / 6 tbsp soft light brown sugar

SERVES 6

38

1 Preheat the oven to 150°C/300°F/Gas 2. Place six 120ml/4fl oz/½ cup ramekins in a roasting tin or ovenproof dish and set aside.

2 Using a small sharp knife, split the vanilla pod lengthways and scrape the black seeds into a pan. Add the pod then add the cream and bring just to the boil over a medium-high heat, stirring frequently. Remove from the heat and cover. Set aside for about 15–20 minutes. Remove the vanilla pod.

3 In a bowl, whisk the egg yolks with the caster sugar and liqueur until well blended. Whisk in the hot cream and strain into a large jug. Divide among the ramekins.

4 Pour enough boiling water into the roasting tin to come halfway up the sides of the ramekin dishes. Cover the tin with foil and bake for about 30 minutes in the preheated oven until the custards are just set. Remove from the tin and leave to cool. Empty the water from the roasting tin, place the ramekins in it again and set aside to chill.

5 Preheat the grill. Sprinkle the soft light brown sugar evenly over the surface of each custard and grill for 30–60 seconds until the sugar melts and caramelizes. (Do not let the sugar burn or the custard curdle.) Place the baked custards in the fridge to set the crust thoroughly and chill the custard completely before serving.

Amaretto Soufflé

INGREDIENTS

6 amaretti biscuits, coarsely crushed
90ml/6 tbsp Amaretto liqueur
4 eggs, separated, plus 1 egg white
115g/4oz/½ cup caster sugar, plus extra
for sprinkling
30ml/2 tbsp plain flour
250ml/8fl oz/1 cup milk
pinch of cream of tartar (optional)
icing sugar, for decorating

SERVES 6

1 Preheat the oven to 200°C/400°F/Gas 6. Butter a 1.5 litre/2½ pint/6 cup soufflé dish; sprinkle with caster sugar. Sprinkle the biscuits with 30ml/2 tbsp of the Amaretto liqueur and set aside.

2 Mix the 4 egg yolks with 30ml/2 tbsp of the caster sugar and the flour. Stir until smooth. Put the milk in a heavy saucepan and heat it just to the boil. Remove from the heat and gradually add the hot milk to the beaten egg mixture, stirring.

3 Pour the milk and egg mixture back into the pan. Set it over a medium-low heat and simmer gently for 4 minutes or until thickened, stirring constantly.

Add the remaining Amaretto liqueur and remove the pan from the heat.

4 In a scrupulously clean, grease-free bowl, whisk the 5 egg whites until they form soft peaks. (If not using a copper bowl, add the cream of tartar as soon as the whites are frothy.) Add the remaining sugar and continue whisking until stiff.

5 Add about one-quarter of the whites to the liqueur mixture and stir in with a rubber spatula. Add the remaining whites and fold in gently.

6 Spoon half the mixture into the prepared dish. Cover with a layer of the moistened amaretti biscuits, then spoon the remaining soufflé mixture evenly on the top.

7 Bake the dish for 20 minutes in the preheated oven or until the soufflé is risen and lightly browned on top. Sprinkle with sifted icing sugar and serve immediately.

Hot Desserts

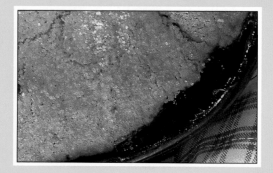

Cherry Batter Pudding

INGREDIENTS

450g/1lb ripe cherries
30ml/2 tbsp kirsch or fruit brandy or
15ml/1 tbsp lemon juice
15ml/1 tbsp icing sugar
45ml/3 tbsp plain flour
45ml/3 tbsp granulated sugar
175ml/6fl oz/¾ cup milk or single cream
2 eggs
grated rind of ½ lemon
pinch of freshly grated nutmeg
1.5ml/¼ tsp vanilla essence

SERVES 4

1 Stone the ripe cherries, if you like. Combine them in a mixing bowl with the kirsch, fruit brandy or lemon juice and icing sugar. Set aside for about 1–2 hours.

2 Preheat the oven to 190°C/375°F/Gas 5. Generously butter a 28cm/11in oval gratin dish or other shallow ovenproof dish.

3 Sift the flour into a bowl. Add the sugar. Slowly whisk in the milk or cream until smoothly blended. Add the eggs, lemon rind, nutmeg and vanilla essence and whisk until well combined and smooth.

4 Scatter the cherries evenly in the baking dish. Pour over the batter and bake in the preheated oven for 45 minutes, or until the pudding is set and puffed around the edges; it is ready when a knife inserted in the centre comes out clean. Serve either warm or at room temperature.

43

Chocolate, Date & Walnut Pudding

INGREDIENTS

25g/1oz/2 tbsp chopped walnuts
25g/1oz/2 tbsp chopped dates
2 eggs
5ml/1 tsp vanilla essence
30ml/2 tbsp golden caster sugar
45ml/3 tbsp wholemeal flour
15ml/1 tbsp cocoa powder
30ml/2 tbsp milk

SERVES 4

1 First, grease a 1.2 litre/2 pint/ 5 cup pudding basin and place a small circle of non-stick baking or greaseproof paper in the base. Spoon in all the chopped walnuts and dates. Preheat the oven to 180°C/350°F/Gas 4.

2 Separate the eggs and place the yolks in a mixing bowl, with the vanilla essence and sugar. Place the bowl over a pan of hot water and whisk until the mixture is thick and pale.

3 Sift the flour and cocoa into the mixture and fold them in with a metal spoon. Stir in the milk, to soften the mixture slightly. Whisk the egg whites until they hold soft peaks and fold them in.

4 Spoon the mixture into the basin and bake for 40–45 minutes, or until risen and firm to the touch. Loosen the edge and turn the pudding out. Serve.

44

Creole Bread & Butter Pudding

INGREDIENTS

4 ready-to-eat dried apricots, chopped
15ml / 1 tbsp raisins
30ml / 2 tbsp sultanas
15ml / 1 tbsp chopped mixed peel
1 French loaf (about 200g / 7oz), thinly sliced
50g / 2oz / 4 tbsp butter, melted
115g / 4oz / ½ cup caster sugar
3 eggs
2.5ml / ½ tsp vanilla essence
475ml / 16fl oz / 2 cups milk
150ml / ¼ pint / ⅔ cup double cream
30ml / 2 tbsp rum
SAUCE
150ml / ¼ pint / ⅔ cup double cream
30ml / 2 tbsp Greek yogurt
15-30ml / 1-2 tbsp rum
15ml / 1 tbsp caster sugar

SERVES 4–6

45

1 Preheat the oven to 180°C/350°F/Gas 4. Lightly butter a deep 1.5 litre/2½ pint/6 cup oven-proof dish. Mix the dried fruits with the mixed peel and sprinkle a little over the base of the dish. Brush both sides of the bread slices with melted butter. Fill the dish with alternate layers of bread and dried fruit, finishing with a layer of bread.

2 Whisk together the sugar, eggs and vanilla essence. Heat the milk and cream until just boiling and whisk into the eggs. Strain over the bread and fruit. Sprinkle the rum on top. Press the bread down, cover with foil and leave for 20 minutes.

3 Bake in a roasting tin half filled with boiling water for 1 hour or until the custard is set. Remove the foil and cook for 10 minutes more, until golden.

4 Warm all the sauce ingredients together in a small pan, stirring gently. Serve with the hot pudding.

Blackberry Cobbler

INGREDIENTS

675g / 1½lb / 6 cups blackberries
225g / 8oz / 1 cup caster sugar
45ml / 3 tbsp plain flour
grated rind of 1 lemon
30ml / 2 tbsp sugar mixed with 1.5ml / ¼ tsp
grated nutmeg
TOPPING
225g / 8oz / 2 cups plain flour
225g / 8oz / 1 cup caster sugar
15ml / 1 tbsp baking powder
1.5ml / ¼ tsp salt
250ml / 8fl oz / 1 cup milk
115g / 4oz / ½ cup butter, melted

SERVES 8

1 First preheat the oven to 180°C/ 350°F/Gas 4. In a mixing bowl, combine all the blackberries with the caster sugar, flour and lemon rind. Stir gently to blend together before transferring to a 2.5 litre/ 4 pint/10 cup ovenproof dish.

2 To make the topping, sift the flour, sugar, baking powder, and salt into a large bowl. Set aside. Combine the milk and butter in a measuring jug.

3 Gradually stir the butter and milk mixture into the dry ingredients in the bowl and stir with a wooden spoon until the batter becomes smooth.

4 Spoon the batter over the fruit mix, spreading it right to the edges. Sprinkle the sugar and nutmeg mixture over the top, then bake in the preheated oven for about 50 minutes, until the batter topping is set and lightly browned. Serve hot.

Apple Soufflé Omelette

48

1 For the filling, gently sauté the apple slices in the butter and sugar until just tender. Stir in the single cream and keep warm, while you make the omelette.

2 Place the egg yolks in a bowl with the cream and sugar and beat well. Whisk the egg whites until stiff, then fold into the yolk mixture.

3 Melt the butter in a large heavy-based frying pan, pour in the soufflé mixture and spread it evenly. Cook for 1 minute until golden underneath, then place under a hot grill and brown the top.

4 Slide the omelette on to a plate, add the apple filling, then fold over. Sift the icing sugar over thickly, then press on a criss-cross pattern with a hot metal skewer. Serve immediately.

INGREDIENTS

4 eggs, separated
30ml / 2 tbsp single cream
15ml / 1 tbsp caster sugar
15g / ½oz / 1 tbsp butter
icing sugar, to decorate
FILLING
1 eating apple, peeled, cored and sliced
25g / 1oz / 2 tbsp butter
30ml / 2 tbsp soft light brown sugar
45ml / 3 tbsp single cream

SERVES 2

COOK'S TIP
For a summer variation, use fresh raspberries or strawberries instead of apples.

Plum Filo Pockets

INGREDIENTS

115g/4oz/½ cup soft cheese
15ml/1 tbsp light muscovado sugar
2.5ml/½ tsp ground cloves
8 large firm plums, halved and stoned
8 sheets filo pastry
sunflower oil, for brushing
icing sugar, to decorate

SERVES 4

1 First, preheat the oven to 220°C/ 425°F/Gas 7 and then mix together the soft cheese, muscovado sugar and cloves in a bowl. Stir well until combined.

2 Sandwich the plum halves back together with a spoonful of the cheese mixture. Spread out the pastry and cut into 16 pieces, about 23cm/9in square. Brush one lightly with oil and place a second on top diagonally. Repeat with the other squares.

3 Put a plum on each pastry square, and pinch the corners together. Put on a baking sheet and bake for 15–18 minutes, until golden. Dust with icing sugar.

Fruity Bread Pudding

2 Quickly remove the pan from the heat and carefully stir in all the diced bread, mixed spice and sliced banana. Mix well. Spoon this mixture into a shallow 1.2 litre/

2 pint/5 cup ovenproof baking dish and then pour the milk over the top in an even layer.

3 Sprinkle the top with the demerara sugar and bake in the hot oven for 25–30 minutes, until it is firm and golden brown. Serve hot or cold, with yogurt.

INGREDIENTS

75g/3oz/½ cup mixed dried fruit
150ml/¼ pint/⅔ cup apple juice
115g/4oz stale brown or white bread, diced
5ml/1 tsp mixed spice
1 large banana, sliced
150ml/¼ pint/⅔ cup milk
15ml/1 tbsp demerara sugar
natural yogurt, to serve

SERVES 4

1 Preheat the oven to 200°C/400°F/Gas 6. Place the dried fruit in a saucepan with the apple juice and bring to the boil.

COOK'S TIP
Different types of bread and its degree of staleness will cause variation in the amount of liquid absorbed, so you may need to adjust the amount of milk to allow for this.

50

Gingerbread Upside Down Pudding

INGREDIENTS

15ml/1 tbsp soft brown sugar
4 peaches, halved and stoned or 8 canned
peach halves
8 walnut halves
yogurt or custard, to serve
BASE
115g/4oz/1 cup wholemeal flour
7.5ml/1½ tsp ground ginger
2.5ml/½ tsp bicarbonate of soda
5ml/1 tsp ground cinnamon
115g/4oz/½ cup demerara sugar
1 egg
120ml/4fl oz/½ cup milk
50ml/2fl oz/¼ cup sunflower oil

SERVES 4–6

2 Arrange the peach halves cut-side down in the tin with a walnut half in each.

3 Make the base. Sift together the flour, ginger, bicarbonate of soda, and cinnamon, then stir in the sugar. Beat together the egg, milk and oil, then mix into the dry ingredients until smooth.

4 Pour the mixture evenly over the peaches and bake for 35–40 minutes, until firm to the touch. Turn out on to a serving plate. Serve hot with yogurt or custard.

51

1 First, preheat the oven to 180°C/ 350°F/Gas 4 and brush the base and sides of a 23cm/ 9in round spring-form tin with oil. Sprinkle the sugar over the base.

Chocolate Desserts

French Chocolate Cake

INGREDIENTS

225g/8oz/1 cup unsalted butter,
cut into pieces
250g/9oz plain chocolate, chopped
115g/4oz/½ cup granulated sugar
30ml/2 tbsp brandy or orange-flavour liqueur
5 eggs
15ml/1 tbsp plain flour
icing sugar, to decorate
sour cream and cherries, to serve

SERVES 10

1 Preheat the oven to 180°C/350°F/Gas 4. Base-line and grease a 23 x 5cm/9 x 2in springform tin. Wrap foil around the tin so it is water-tight.

2 Stir the butter, the chocolate and sugar over a low heat until smooth. Cool slightly. Stir in the liqueur. In a mixing bowl, beat the eggs lightly, then beat in the flour. Slowly beat in the chocolate mixture until blended. Pour into the tin, smoothing the surface.

3 Place the springform tin in a roasting tin and pour in boiling water to come 2cm/¾in up the side of the springform tin. Bake for 25–30 minutes until the edge of the cake is set, but the centre is still soft. Remove the foil. Cool in the tin on a wire rack (the cake will sink and may crack).

4 Turn the cake on to a wire rack. Remove the springform tin bottom and paper, so the bottom of the cake is now the top.

5 Cut 6–8 strips of non-stick baking paper 2.5cm/1in wide and place them randomly over the cake, or make a lattice-style pattern if you wish. Dust the cake with icing sugar, then carefully remove the paper. Slide the cake on to a serving plate and serve with sour cream and fresh cherries.

Luxury White Chocolate Cheesecake

INGREDIENTS

150g/5oz (about 16-18) digestive biscuits
50g/2oz/½ cup blanched hazelnuts, toasted
50g/2oz/4 tbsp unsalted butter, melted
2.5ml/½ tsp ground cinnamon
FILLING
350g/12oz fine quality white chocolate, chopped
120ml/4fl oz/½ cup whipping or
double cream
675g/1½lb/3 x 8oz packets cream
cheese, softened
50g/2oz/¼ cup granulated sugar
4 eggs
15ml/1 tbsp vanilla essence
TOPPING
450ml/¾ pint/scant 2 cups soured cream
50g/2oz/¼ cup granulated sugar
15ml/1 tbsp hazelnut-flavour liqueur or
5ml/1 tsp vanilla essence
white chocolate curls, to decorate
cocoa, for dusting (optional)

SERVES 16–20

1 Preheat the oven to 180°C/350°F/Gas 4 and grease a 23 x 7.5cm/9 x 3in springform tin. Process the biscuits and hazelnuts to fine crumbs, then mix with the butter and cinnamon. Press the mixture on to the bottom and sides of the tin and bake for 5–7 minutes, or until just set.

2 Lower the oven to 150°C/300°F/Gas 2. Make the filling. Melt the chocolate and cream over a low heat until smooth, stirring frequently. Cool.

3 Beat the cream cheese and sugar until smooth; beat in the eggs, one at a time, the white chocolate mixture and vanilla. Pour into the baked crust and bake for  45–55 minutes, or until the edge of the filling is firm but the centre is still slightly soft. Transfer to a wire rack, still in its tin, and increase the oven to 200°C/400°F/Gas 6.

4 Make the topping. Whisk the soured cream with the sugar and liqueur or vanilla and pour it over the cheesecake, spreading it evenly. Return the cheesecake to the oven for 5–7 minutes. Turn off the oven, but do not open the door for 1 hour.

5 Transfer the cheesecake to a wire rack to cool in the tin. Remove the tin, then chill the cheesecake, loosely covered, overnight.

6 Place the cheesecake on a serving plate. Decorate the top with chocolate curls and dust lightly with cocoa, if liked.

Chocolate Pavlova with Chocolate Curls

INGREDIENTS

275g/10oz/2½ cups icing sugar
15ml/1 tbsp unsweetened cocoa
5ml/1 tsp cornflour
5 egg whites, at room temperature
pinch of salt
5ml/1 tsp cider vinegar or lemon juice
CHOCOLATE CREAM
175g/6oz plain chocolate, chopped
120ml/4fl oz/½ cup milk
25g/1oz/2 tbsp butter, diced
30ml/2 tbsp brandy
475ml/16fl oz/2 cups double cream
TOPPING
450g/1lb/4 cups mixed berries or diced
mango, papaya, lychees and pineapple
chocolate curls
icing sugar

SERVES 8–10

1 Preheat the oven to 160°C/325°F/Gas 3. Place a sheet of non-stick baking paper on to a baking sheet and mark a 20cm/8in circle on it. Sift 45ml/3 tbsp of the icing sugar with the cocoa and cornflour and set aside. Using an electric mixer, beat the egg whites until frothy. Add the salt and beat until the whites form stiff peaks.

2 Sprinkle the remaining icing sugar into the egg whites, a little at a time, making sure each addition is dissolved before beating in the next. Fold in the cornflour mixture, then quickly fold in the vinegar or lemon juice.

3 Now spoon the mixture on to the paper circle, with the sides higher than the centre. Bake for 1 hour, until set, then turn off the oven but leave the meringue

inside for 1 hour longer. Remove from the oven, peel off the paper and leave to cool.

4 Make the chocolate cream. Melt the chocolate and milk over a low heat, stirring until smooth. Remove from the heat and whisk in the butter and brandy. Cool for 1 hour.

5 Transfer the meringue to a serving plate. When the chocolate mixture has cooled, but is not too firm, beat the cream until soft peaks form. Stir half the cream into the chocolate mixture to lighten it, then fold in the remaining cream. Spoon it into the centre of the meringue. Arrange fruit and chocolate curls in the centre of the meringue, over the cream. Dust with icing sugar.

Chocolate Cream Puffs

INGREDIENTS

250ml/8fl oz/1 cup water
2.5ml/½ tsp salt
15ml/1 tbsp granulated sugar
115g/4oz/½ cup unsalted butter, diced
150g/5oz/1¼ cups plain flour, sifted
30ml/2 tbsp unsweetened cocoa, sifted
4-5 eggs
1 quantity Chocolate Cream (page 62),
for filling
GLAZE
300ml/½ pint/1¼ cups whipping cream
50g/2oz/4 tbsp unsalted butter, diced
15ml/1 tbsp corn or golden syrup
225g/8oz plain chocolate, chopped
5ml/1 tsp vanilla essence

MAKES 12

1 Preheat the oven to 220°C/425°F/Gas 7. Grease a baking sheet. Bring the water, salt, sugar and butter to the boil. Remove from the heat; tip in the flour and cocoa. Stir vigorously until the mixture leaves the sides of the pan. Cook for 1 minute, beating constantly. Remove from the heat.

2 Beat in four of the eggs, one at a time. The mixture should be thick, smooth and shiny and fall from a spoon. If it is too dry, beat the fifth egg and beat it into the mixture gradually. Spoon the batter into an icing bag with a star tip and pipe 12 puffs on the prepared baking sheet.

3 Bake the puffs for 35–40 minutes until puffed and firm. Slice off the top third of each puff and return both tops and bottoms, cut-side up, to the baking sheet. Cook for a few minutes more, to dry out. Cool on a wire rack.

4 Spoon the chocolate cream into a piping bag fitted with a plain tip. Fill the bottom of each puff, then cover with a top.

5 Make the glaze. Melt the cream, butter, syrup, chocolate and vanilla until smooth, stirring often. Remove from the heat and leave to cool for about 20–30 minutes, until slightly thickened. Pour a little glaze over each of the cream puffs, or dip the top of each puff into the glaze, and leave to set. To serve, arrange the puffs on a serving plate in a single layer or pile them up on top of each other.

Chocolate Loaf with Coffee Sauce

INGREDIENTS

175g/6oz plain chocolate, chopped
50g/2oz/4 tbsp butter, softened
4 large eggs, separated
30ml/2 tbsp rum or brandy (optional)
pinch of cream of tartar
chocolate curls and chocolate coffee beans,
to decorate
COFFEE SAUCE
600ml/1 pint/2½ cups milk
9 egg yolks
50g/2oz/¼ cup caster sugar
5ml/1 tsp vanilla essence
15ml/1 tbsp instant coffee powder, dissolved
in 30ml/2 tbsp hot water

SERVES 6–8

1 Line a 1.2 litre/2 pint/5 cup loaf tin with clear film. Place the plain chocolate in a bowl set over hot water and leave for 3–5 minutes, then stir.

2 Remove the bowl from the pan and quickly beat in the butter, egg yolks, one at a time, and rum or brandy, if using.

3 In a clean grease-free bowl, using an electric mixer, beat the egg whites slowly until frothy. Add the cream of tartar, increase the speed and continue beating until they form soft peaks, then stiffer peaks that just flop over a little. Stir one-third of the egg whites into the chocolate mixture, then fold in the remaining whites. Pour into the lined loaf tin and smooth the top. Cover and freeze until ready to serve.

4 Make the coffee sauce. Bring the milk to a simmer over a medium heat. Whisk the egg yolks and the sugar for 2–3 minutes until thick and creamy, then whisk in the hot milk and return the mixture to the saucepan. With a wooden spoon, stir over a low heat until the sauce begins to thicken and coat the back of the spoon. Strain the custard into a chilled bowl, stir in the vanilla essence and coffee and set aside to cool, stirring occasionally. Chill.

5 To serve, uncover the loaf tin and dip the base into hot water for 10 seconds. Invert the chocolate loaf on to a board and peel off the clear film. Cut the loaf into slices and serve with the coffee sauce. Decorate with the chocolate curls and chocolate coffee beans.

Hazelnut Meringue Torte with Pears

INGREDIENTS

175g/6oz/¾ cup granulated sugar
1 vanilla pod, split
475ml/16fl oz/2 cups water
4 ripe pears, peeled, halved and cored
6 egg whites
275g/10oz/2½ cups icing sugar
175g/6oz/1¼ cups ground hazelnuts
5ml/1 tsp vanilla essence
50g/2oz plain chocolate, melted
chocolate caraque, to decorate
CHOCOLATE CREAM
475ml/16fl oz/2 cups whipping cream
275g/10oz plain chocolate, melted
60ml/4 tbsp hazelnut-flavour liqueur

SERVES 8–10

1 In a pan large enough to hold the pears in a single layer, combine the sugar, vanilla pod and water. Bring to the boil, stirring until the sugar dissolves. Reduce the heat and add the pears. Cover and simmer for 12–15 minutes until tender. Remove from heat and leave to cool. Preheat the oven to 180°C/350°F/Gas 4.

2 Draw a 23cm/9in circle on two sheets of non-stick baking paper and place on two baking sheets.

3 Whisk the egg whites until soft peaks form then gradually add the icing sugar, whisking until stiff and glossy. Gently fold in the nuts and vanilla and spoon the meringue on to the marked circles. Bake for 1 hour. Turn off the heat and cool in the oven.

4 Slice the pear halves lengthways. Make the chocolate cream. Beat the cream to soft peaks, then fold in the melted chocolate and liqueur. Put a third of the chocolate cream into an icing bag fitted with a star tip. Spread one meringue layer with half the remaining chocolate cream and top with half the pears. Pipe rosettes around the edge.

5 Top with the second meringue and the remaining chocolate cream and pear slices. Pipe rosettes around the edge. Drizzle the melted chocolate over the pears and decorate with the chocolate caraque. Chill for 1 hour before serving.

Index